We hope this will bring happy .....
until you are here again!
Much love from Jan

THE SPIRIT

OF

EAST ANGLIA

Greetings from

....

Published by Heritage House (Publishers) Limited
Steam Mill Road, Bradfield, Manningtree, CO11 2QT
www.heritage-house.co.uk e-mail: sales@heritage-house.co.uk
Sketches © Jill Raeburn Wilson 2004
Poems © Jane Shepherd-Miller 2004
ISBN 1-85215-0645

THE SPIRIT

OF

EAST ANGLIA

Sketches by Jill Raeburn Wilson
Poems by Jane Shepherd-Miller

Heritage House (Publishers) Limited
2004

CONTENTS

INTRODUCTION

The very idea of the book creates a wonderful picture of these two good friends, Jane and Jill, travelling East Anglia, sketching the pockets that appeal to them and later, in the quiet of an evening, putting words to their pictures. The end result is an utterly charming book full of drawings of well-known areas as well as quiet corners of this lovely part of England. The poetry that accompanies the artwork is as fresh as the breeze from the North Sea.

This little collection will be enjoyed by East Anglians and visitors alike.

John Talman

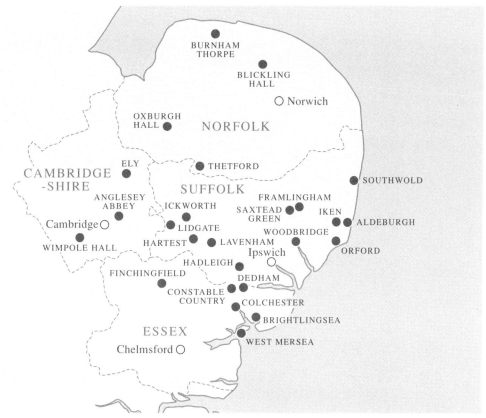

BURNHAM THORPE

BLICKLING HALL

○ Norwich

OXBURGH HALL

NORFOLK

ELY

CAMBRIDGE -SHIRE

THETFORD

SUFFOLK

SOUTHWOLD

ANGLESEY ABBEY

ICKWORTH

FRAMLINGHAM

SAXTEAD GREEN

IKEN

ALDEBURGH

Cambridge ○

LIDGATE

WOODBRIDGE

WIMPOLE HALL

HARTEST

LAVENHAM

ORFORD

Ipswich ○

HADLEIGH

FINCHINGFIELD

DEDHAM

CONSTABLE COUNTRY

COLCHESTER

ESSEX

BRIGHTLINGSEA

Chelmsford ○

WEST MERSEA

Based on Ordnance Survey mapping with permission of HMSO.Crown copyright (MC100020020)

Colchester Castle

From Romans to Normans and then Civil War
Here stands a castle from ruins before
Camulodunum oldest of all English towns
But never the host of a past monarch crowned

That is apart from our Queen Boudica
Who ruled her town proudly with heiress daughter
The Romans dared challenge this bountiful Queen
Who banished them smartly, her power redeemed

The Romans returned though for 400 years
'Til the Temple of Claudius caused hatred and jeers
Since then Norman Conquerors built up its walls
And Colchester Castle it came to be called

No battle was fought under castle's huge Keep
But lay siege to the Royalists before their defeat
Cromwell's men shot Lisle and Lucas at wall
And then came the Plague where 4,000 did fall

And now stands the Castle near playground and park
And the ghosts of the past rest within the walls dark

Colchester Castle

13-5-03

Iken Church

Harsh Winter falls on virgin buds
Soon to screen promontory
Thames barge weaves on high tide through mud –
making its way along the estuary.

Distant dormant village early morn
Still chill the frosted sleeping blades of grass
Grey cumulus comes creeping up since dawn
And Saxon church bells ring the ages passed

Iken Church

6-3-03

Ely Cathedral

Sky streaked cloud over cold and windswept field
Blown and bare stand branches on the tree
Sturdy curlew braces, graceful grasslands yield
And in far distance rises high Ely

Brave Etheldreda, Saxon Queen, her monastery long gone
Monks once heralded then dissolved to live in fear
Now priests abide to keep the legacy on
Of this fine mantle over Cambridgeshire

Great ship of the Fens steers worship to God the Son
And welcomes aboard all visitors to this place
Lady Chapel, Priory, Nave, Fine Octagon
Give Peace, Rest and Love through His eternal Grace

Ely Cathedral   8-4-03

Framlingham Castle

Across the marshland in the distance
Rises Framlingham Castle, solid, fortified
Stark twelfth century origins made grander
With prison tower and Tudor chimneys applied

From here as Queen, Mary Tudor went forth
In July of the year 1553
Bloody, vengeful she restored her Faith
With punishment and cruelty

Framlingham Castle

7·5·03

Lidgate

Lidgate picturesque waterside village
All lanes wind up to Commanding Heart
Of worship, striking Norman bell tower
Summoning Christians to play their part.

St Mary's the marriage of ancient and modern
Crafted, refined, beatified, enlarged
Sturdy steadfast solid great walls
Where Pilgrims' Holy love is carved

As banks drift down to village pond
Where Nature softens Winter to Spring
Another cycle of life eternal
Through mother ducks and ducklings

Lidgate

16~4~03

Little Hall, Lavenham

What long forgotten memories
Held here within the beams?
Of baker, parson, country squire
Or courting youth so lean?
Aged craggy carved outline
Silhouettes the sky
Still you stand in our time
Watching passers-by

Little Hall, Lavenham

16-11-02

Oxburgh Hall

Oxburgh Hall, towering imposing manor
A palpable history of triumph and candour
Host to King Henry and Elizabeth his wife
Whose marriage united the rose Red and White
Noble Bedingfeld family dissenters from State
Hid their priests in a Hole to receive blessings and wait
For hard times to soften on Catholic's death knell
But for whom a conversion would bring death unto Hell
Their stalwart defences played down lest they bring
Unwanted attention from the Protestant King
The left spiral staircase, moat, stone crenellations
Subtle, discreet but strong innovations

Once more at peace but to help pay State duty
The Public can pay to admire all its beauty
Now Summer's eve sketched in this picture frame
Shows the hall enjoying a more slumbersome reign

Oxburgh Hall   21-7-03

The Crown Inn, Hartest

Wherever you may wander
Throughout the British land
You cannot miss the familiar sign
Of a Public House at hand

It really is a wonder
Of varied hops and beers
The clank of feet on wooden boards
And people saying 'CHEERS!'

This elegant example
So very picturesque
A pub but also country inn
Once Manor of Hartest

Whether posh or spit and sawdust
The ubiquitous English pub
Offers ale and rest to a thirsty guest
And serves up hearty grub

The Crown Inn, Hartest

15-5-03

Anglesey Abbey

High windows grand look out to see
a cacophony of scenery.
Lead-latticed panes, arched-oak door
embrace fine lawns and trees before.
Listen, can you hear the trill
Of blackbird, thrush and skylark still?

Tall chimneys smokeless now reflect
Past grandeur - but do not neglect
The grace of style and life withal
Solid, enduring within these walls
Silent, prayerful men did wander
Through the halls and garden yonder

Anglesey Abbey

15/7/02

Orford

Orford – avenue, tranquil homesteads
disguise the ominous coast nearby
inhospitable bleak and wasted
rough seas echo dead sailors' cries

Where leaded windows' welcome lights
shine home the weary workers' day
yon chill shore wind of Winter-night
dares lone mortals to pass its way

Orford   27-1-03

River Brett, Hadleigh

Packhorse-bridge a solid reminder
Of journeys long, not hours but days
Cattle herded and driven to market
Along windy Suffolk byways

A major thoroughfare no longer
The bridge creates a pleasant scene
Rising over the willow-waters
Still, reflecting, nature serene

River Brett, Hadleigh

24-9-02

Blickling Hall

No humble abode, no modest nest
This grand Hall was designed to impress
Tower, wings impregnable-walls so high
Its powerful silhouette, ominous, imposing
On the hapless visitor or passer-by

Unchanged the east wall masterfully towers
O'er the old parterre now carved with borders and flowers
The formal hedges, topiary trees, font and urn,
Where here storm clouds gather darkly menacing,
Like giant chess pieces wait their turn

As if to stand still defending, ready
And like ghostly soldiers holding eternal, steady
The birthright of their masters' distinguished family tree,
A sensitive sketch captures a phantom battlefield
Symbolic protest to modernity

Blickling Hall   30·7·03

Wimpole Hall, view from terrace

Gazing from the terrace of this magnificent pile
The largest home in Cambridgeshire to date
Behind, the interior's pedigree in grandest style
Beyond a snapshot of the grounds within the gates

No Chinese bridge, grand folly or lake here do we see
But gaze upon this charming land in Spring
Behold the cherry blossom, Narcissi, spiral topiary
And then sheep grazing, what pleasure to the eye they bring

Wimpole Hall – view from terrace

22-4-03

Statue of Thomas Paine, Thetford

He stands defiant in stone like a celestial archer
Quill pen deftly poised to fire freethinking arrow
Penetrating men's hearts, revolutionary father –
New World Independence, imperialism overthrow

Challenger of Faith, patriot of people not of law
'My own mind is my Church', equality of man, his honest creed
Spurning personal gain he gave to the poor
But was shunned and reviled for sacrilegious screed

'He had lived long did some good and much harm' it said
When destitute in New York City he passed away
No Englishman, but here in Thetford born and bred
And yet oblivious still today's folk go their way.

Statue of Thomas Paine, Thetford   9-7-03

The Tide Mill, Woodbridge

Rocking gently on the windless water
Katriana's cargo-kin home moored at the bay
Toiling no more the weatherboard tide mill slumbers
After the busy working yesterdays
A craft beyond Katriana kills the frame
Where way back our imaginations may have led
When great stones would be grinding still the grain
As they for centuries milled folk's daily bread

Now tranquil in this windless mid-May morn
Where this mill would till by moon and tide
Modern technology this way of life might scorn
But here glimpse history lovingly restored, revived

The Tide Mill, Woodbridge

KATRIANA

6-5-03

Heat-wave at Ickworth

Gentleman of Bristol, your day is done
But your collectables at Ickworth live on
Rich, eccentric, 18th Century Earl
Titian, Gainsborough, Velazquez – the pearl
of your vast wealth.

Woodland walks, Deer Enclosure, Vineyard, Italian garden
Central rotunda, curved corridors, magnificent silver.
All treasures on display without pardon

Today ordinary folk can pay and enter
And gawp with wonder at this opulent centre.
A heat-wave shimmers over avenue hedge
And tourists admire from the Palladian ledge.

Heatwave at Ickworth   17/6/02

The Post Mill, Saxtead Green

Great sails stand atrophied only turning for the tourist trade,
Like the Lords of Framlingham Castle a lifestyle now in history laid.
No longer needed to grind for the privileged few
The massive sails stand over this most impressive view
White weatherboard wonderful ancient windmill grand
Stands firm and strong and proud looking over this windswept land.

Saxtead Green Post Mill   9-2-04

All Saints, Burnham Thorpe

Soporific birdsong in balmy Summer heat
Gentle breeze rustles a luscious tree.
Within sways soft his ensign of the fleet
'Pole ropes grind together as if on ship at sea.
Suddenly – the mind drifts awake to battles
To great sail ships fore and aft afire
Men shouting, dying as cannon ball rattles
Urged on by their hero in full battle attire
Horatio Lord Nelson, great leader of men
Patriot with passion proud self-sacrifice
Remembered with reverence now, greatly loved then.
Wooden cross crafted from VICTORY where he lost his life.

In London a hero's statue upon Column so high
Yet here a family's memories around the church lie

All Saints, Burnham Thorpe   14-7-03

The Lighthouse, Southwold

There stands the lighthouse brilliant white against a deep blue sky
And behold the row of elegant houses
Quietly stand – the occasional passer-by

Warmly wrapped against this crisp-cold winter's noon
Walking purposefully not even strolling
Hastening as shadows fade, to avoid the gloom

Sleepy Southwold seaside slumbers same throughout the ages
From modest hamlet to wealthy fishing port
The sea has determined its many stages

No grand sights does it offer, no cathedral, castle, ruin or rail
Just that quiet confidence of age withstanding
Any intrusion, whether human or weather gale.

The Lighthouse, Southwold

25 - 1 - 04

Brightlingsea

Tall ships and Clipper homeward came
And lined the harbour pool
Hustle, bustle an industry thrived
On trade of cloth and wool

Tired Colne banks now your heyday gone
Bleak docks where children play
Small craft, dinghies, quietly anchored
On ghostly loading bay

Brightlingsea

27-9-02

Aldeburgh

Fishing tackle, fishing nets
Huts nearby collect the cull
Viking, Blind Faith, Challenger
Emblazoned on their hull

These clues stand in honour
Of old craft, by no means through
Not abandoned but awaiting
The sea's harvest anew

Aldeburgh   4-10-02

Finchingfield

First behold the Church tower
Christian bastion in our midst
Then the houses irregular
Cottage gardens' dew sun-kissed

And then the verdant lushness
Of the well kept village green
And last the looming crucifix
On the War memorial seen

REMEMBER – *folk here won't forget*
Young soldiers gave their lives
In two Great Wars successive
So that Englishness survives

Finchingfield

28-3-03

Dedham Mill

Luxury apartments, penthouse vast
Some find their dream home here at last.
Rural setting, peaceful, still
What's become of Dedham Mill?

Giant blades rot where waters once would flow
To generate energy years ago
Where country folk would grind the grain
Such times never seen again
Great mill stands elegant, sublime
Not ravaged by the passing time

Secret Garden, Constable Country

Lady standing all alone
Was this once your treasured home?
Does the gate that let you in
Stay open for your spirit kin?
East Anglia where ghostly tale
Is shared by folk enjoying ale.
Do you stand a grey foreboding
amidst the summer flower exploding?

High Tide, West Mersea

Boats, lie still and anchored
Gently rocking on the tide

Telegraph poles, loom defiant
In the marsh – their lines have died

Sky, grey storm clouds gather
To hasten waiting dusk

Birds, fly frantic searching
For lugworm or mollusc

Marshland eve setting in
Seasons passing, quiet spirits within

High tide, West Mersea

10-10-02